This book belongs to:

. . . .

. . . .

Editor: Carly Madden
Designer: Hannah Mason
Series Designer: Victoria Kimonidou
Editorial Director: Victoria Garrard
Art Director: Laura Roberts-Jensen

Copyright © QED Publishing 2015
First published in the UK in 2015
by QED Publishing
Part of The Quarto Group
The Old Brewery
6 Blundell Street
London N7 9BH
www.qed-publishing.co.uk

A catalogue record for this book is available from the British Library.

ISBN 978 1 78493 127 8

Printed in China

Get Some Rest,
Sleeping
Beauty!

Written by **Steve Smallman**

Illustrated by **Neil Price**

Once upon a time in a land far away, a king and queen held a party for their beautiful baby daughter, Aurora.

The guests of honour were five fairies, who each gave the baby magical gifts.

I give her the gift
of imagination!
POOF!

I give her the gift
of cleverness!
POOF!

I give her
the gift
of music!
POOF!

I give her
the gift
of dance!
POOF!

The last fairy
was just about to
give her gift to
the baby when...

..."STOP!"

An evil fairy appeared,
looking very cross.

"I see you didn't
invite me!"
she shrieked.

The fairy gave an evil cackle and said,

"Here's my gift for the baby. When Aurora turns sixteen, she'll prick her finger on the needle of a spinning wheel...

...and go to sleep for ever and ever!"

Then the fairy vanished in a puff of smelly smoke.

The last fairy still
had her gift to give.

"I can't stop the curse,"
she said...

..."but I can change it
so that the princess falls
asleep for a hundred
years instead. She will
be awoken by a kiss
from a prince."

The king and queen immediately banned all spinning wheels from the kingdom to try to avoid the curse.

They didn't want their daughter to sleep for a hundred years, but in fact...

...Princess Aurora didn't like sleeping at all!

When she was a baby she kept her parents up all night, crying very loudly.

As she got older,
Aurora just
didn't want to
go to sleep.

When her mum
and dad told her
to go to bed,
she ignored them!

Aurora stayed up late
every night, playing games,
reading, bouncing on
her bed and having
midnight feasts.

She was always very tired and
grumpy the next morning.

The more tired Aurora became,
the grumpier she got!

She shouted at everyone
who came near her.

People started calling her
Aurora the Roarer
behind her back and she
had no friends.

Not only that,
she had big bags
under her eyes and
was so clumsy!

She was always dropping
things, breaking things
and bumping into things.

On her sixteenth birthday, Aurora was moaning about having to get up. As usual!

Her mum said, "Don't be grumpy on your birthday, darling."

"I AM NOT GRUMPY!" Aurora bellowed.

She stomped through the castle until she came across a room that she'd never seen before.

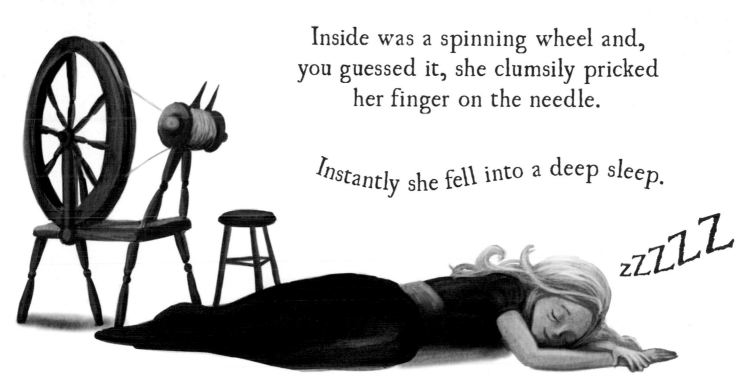

Inside was a spinning wheel and, you guessed it, she clumsily pricked her finger on the needle.

Instantly she fell into a deep sleep.

zZZZZ

A fairy heard Aurora's loud snores and moved her into her comfy bed.

Then she waved her wand and made everyone else in the castle fall asleep too!

Huge, thorny bushes grew up
and buried the castle,
where it lay undisturbed
for years and years.

The story about a bad-tempered, enchanted princess who'd
been sent to sleep for a hundred years spread across the land.

One hundred years later,
a handsome prince
turned up. He wanted to
see if the story was true.

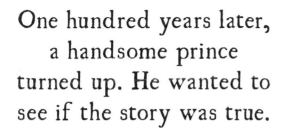

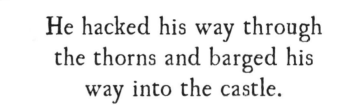

He hacked his way through
the thorns and barged his
way into the castle.

He found Aurora lying in bed
and gasped in surprise!

She looked so calm
and peaceful. The prince
kissed her and...

POOF!

...she woke up!

Aurora felt wonderful!
She didn't look grumpy and had
no bags under her eyes either.

"What a lovely sleep," she sighed.
"Ooh, hello, have we met?"

Everybody else in the castle woke up too.

The king and queen were amazed at how bright,
happy and healthy their daughter was.

"She just needed a good sleep,"
said the queen. "We all did!"

Aurora hugged her parents
and said sorry for being
so grumpy before.

She promised that she'd always make
sure she had a good night's sleep.

Aurora married the prince and was so happy that nobody ever called her Aurora the Roarer again.

But sometimes they called her **Aurora the Snorer** instead!

Next steps

Show the children the cover again. When they first saw it, did they think that they already knew the story? How is this story different from the traditional story? Which bits are the same?

Aurora didn't sleep very well when she was a baby. Ask the children if they know any babies who don't sleep at night. Do the babies get grumpy? Do their mums and dads get grumpy too?

Aurora hated going to bed and always stayed up late. Ask the children if they have ever stayed up really late. Did they feel tired the next day? Why do the children think it's important to get enough sleep?

Aurora got very clumsy because she was tired all the time and she was so grumpy that she didn't have any friends. Ask the children how they would feel if they were like Aurora.

When Aurora finally woke up after her very long sleep, how did she feel? Ask the children how they feel when they've had a lovely long sleep.

Aurora snored when she was asleep. Ask the children to draw a picture of somebody fast asleep and snoring! Tip: eyes shut, mouth open and a long line of Zs!